IMAGES
of London

LONDON'S RAILWAYS

IMAGES
of London

LONDON'S
RAILWAYS

K.A. Scholey

TEMPUS

First published 1999
Reprinted 2004

Tempus Publishing Limited
The Mill, Brimscombe Port,
Stroud, Gloucestershire, GL5 2QG
www.tempus-publishing.com

British Library Cataloguing in Publication Data.
A catalogue record for this book is available from the British Library.

ISBN 0 7524 1605 7

Typesetting and origination by Tempus Publishing Limited.
Printed in Great Britain.

Contents

Introduction   7

1. London's Termini   11

2. North London Railway   45

3. Metropolitan and District Railways   57

4. The Tubes   73

5. The Tuppenny Tube   87

6. London's Other Stations   95

7. North Western Suburban   109

dedicated to my grandfather
Arthur William Baker

Introduction

In the nineteenth century London was the most important city in the world, the capital of an empire 'on which the sun never set'. This was the golden age of railway building and this is reflected in the city's transport history and infrastructure. London has more main line stations than any other city, was the first city to have an underground railway, the first to have an underground electric railway and now has one of the largest underground railway systems in the world. The city can even claim to have the world's first public railway, the Surrey Iron Railway. All these factors make it of primary interest to railway history enthusiasts.

Although images dating from 1850 to 1950 are included, the main aim is to provide a cross section of railway activity in London during the Edwardian era – the height of the railway age. Because of their paramount interest, London's termini are covered in some depth, as are suburban lines and the underground. Other aspects of railway life not usually seen by the public, such as goods traffic, much of which has now totally vanished, are also shown.

The origins of Britain's railways are commercial. Lines were authorized by Parliament but built and run by private enterprise. The first railways in the 1820s and 1830s were isolated pioneers. Their success lead to a flurry of schemes that culminated in the so-called Railway Mania of 1844-46. By 1914 the railway network was at its largest, with around 130 companies, some large, some very small indeed. The companies were contemporarily referred to by a shortened version of their full title (thus the London & South Western became the 'South Western') or by their initials (e.g. LSWR). The financial strain of the First World War on the companies made them more amenable to reorganization by the government and 'Grouping' took place in 1923. On this date the individual companies were arranged into four large entities, which remained private concerns. These were the Great Western (GWR), Southern (SR), London Midland & Scottish (LMS) and London & North Eastern (LNER). Overuse and lack of essential maintenance during the Second World War caused financial problems. In 1948 the almost bankrupt railway companies were nationalized. During the 1960s and early 1970s the railway network was severely curtailed – the infamous Beeching era. This, however, did not severely affect London. British Railways, as the nationalized network was termed, lasted until privatization in the mid-1990s.

An exception to the pattern outlined above can be found in London. The local concerns that were later to become the London Underground of today also started as private

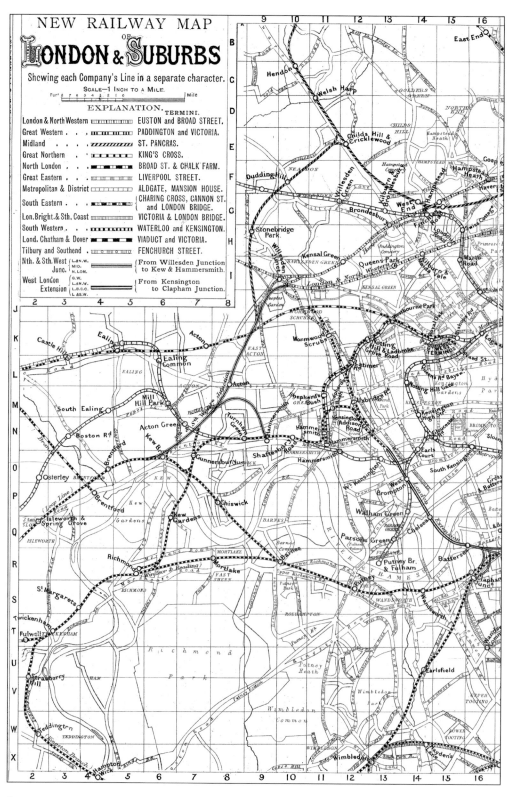

NEW RAILWAY MAP
OF
LONDON & SUBURBS

Showing each Company's Line in a separate character.

SCALE—1 INCH TO A MILE.

EXPLANATION.

TERMINI.

London & North Western . . . . EUSTON and BROAD STREET.
Great Western . . . . PADDINGTON and VICTORIA.
Midland . . . . ST. PANCRAS.
Great Northern . . . . KING'S CROSS.
North London . . . . BROAD ST. & CHALK FARM.
Great Eastern . . . . LIVERPOOL STREET.
Metropolitan & District . . . . ALDGATE, MANSION HOUSE.
South Eastern . . . . CHARING CROSS, CANNON ST. and LONDON BRIDGE.
Lon. Bright.& Sth. Coast . . . . VICTORIA & LONDON BRIDGE.
South Western . . . . WATERLOO and KENSINGTON.
Lond. Chatham & Dover . . . . VIADUCT and VICTORIA.
Tilbury and Southend . . . . FENCHURCH STREET.
Nth. & Sth. West Junc. { L.&N.W. N.LON. } From Willesden Junction to Kew & Hammersmith.
West London Extension { G.W. L.&N.W. L.B.&C. L.&S.W. } From Kensington to Clapham Junction.

8

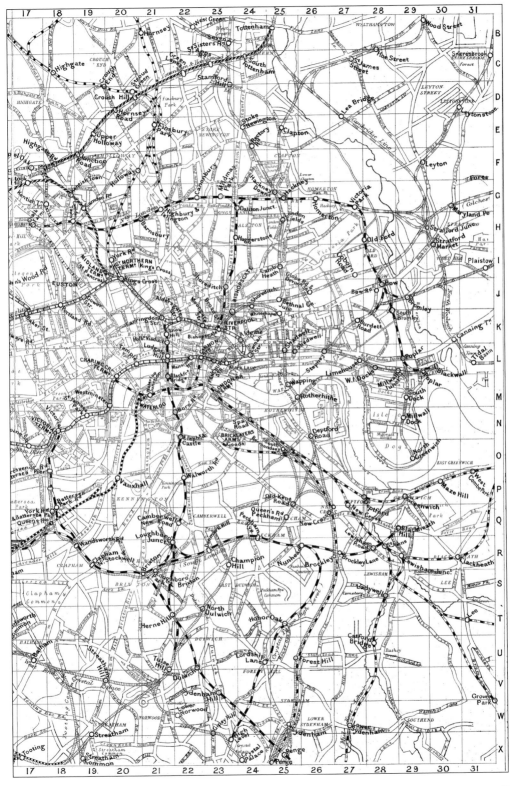

companies. The first, the Metropolitan Railway, originated as a link between termini, but soon spread beyond suburbia into rural backwaters. The 'Met' and its contemporary, the District Railway, ran large profile (initially steam) trains in shallow tunnels and cuttings. Really efficient transport in inner London had to await the advent of the tubes – all electric, deep-bored tunnels – in the 1890s. The first of these was the City and South London Railway – the world's first underground electric railway. By 1914 most of the tubes and the District had been taken over by a company usually referred to as the Underground group. Both the Underground group and the still independent Metropolitan survived Grouping only to be combined as London Transport under the control of local (later national) government in 1933.

The companies that operated in London are indicated on the map on the previous pages. As this map (not wholly accurate) dates from 1884, there were some important later additions – principally the arrival of the Great Central in 1899 (see page 128) and the building of the tube railways (between 1890 and 1910). Other important changes were the effective amalgamation of the South Eastern and the London, Chatham & Dover in 1899 to form the South Eastern & Chatham Railway, and the swallowing of the London, Tilbury & Southend by the Midland in 1912. A grid reference relating to the map is given where relevant.

Many of the images in this selection reflect the varied architecture of London's stations. By limiting the use of views featuring rolling stock, I hope to appeal to all Londoners and not just 'train buffs'. Railways were, and still are, a part of everyday life in the same way as the car is – a part of social history and an integral part of the fabric of society.

The majority of the images in this book are from picture postcards. Old postcards are one of the major sources for the pictorial history of the early twentieth century. The first illustrated postcards in Britain were issued in 1894 but the craze for sending and collecting them did not take off until 1902. The golden age of the picture postcard was ended by the First World War since the majority of postcards were printed in Germany.

Of course this short book is far from being comprehensive – further reference works include:

R. Davies & M.D. Grant, *London and its railways*, David & Charles
H.V. Borley, *Chronology of London Railways*, Railway & Canal Historical Society
A.A. Jackson, *London's Termini*, David & Charles
A.A. Jackson, *London's Local Railways*, David & Charles
A.A. Jackson & D.F. Croome, *Rails through the clay*, George Allen & Unwin

One
London's Termini

London's termini are a mixed bunch of buildings: from St Pancras, sublime, to Broad Street, ridiculous. Most, however, are middling in quality – neither phenomenally good nor atrociously bad. In this lies the significance of London's stations as typical Victorian buildings. However, stations are not mere brick and iron architecture; they are hives of activity where goes on the toing and froing that helps make London such an interesting and cosmopolitan city. Each station has an individual personality comprised of many elements including its physical nature, the character of the company which built it and the people who use it.

Paddington

Paddington (ref: K 15). London terminus of the Great Western Railway, the route to South Wales and the West of England, Paddington is one of the world's great stations. Its cathedral-like train-shed was the first of its kind and widely imitated. The decorated ends of the shed are perhaps the most fascinating feature of the building and are a clear precursor of the *Art Nouveau* style that was to start some forty-odd years later. The Great Western Hotel fronts the station.

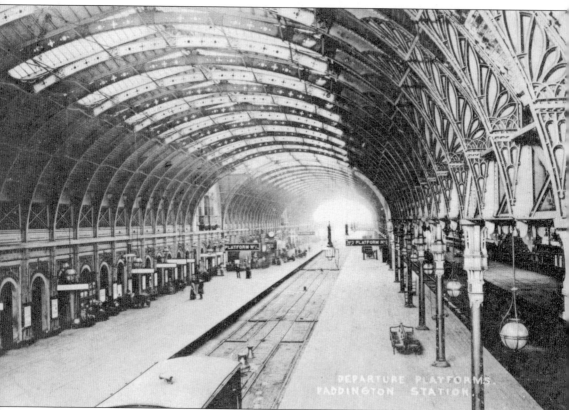

The platforms, *c.*1904. The magnificent train halls, probably the best in London, were the work of Isambard Kingdom Brunel and Matthew Digby Wyatt. Each of the three original spans is 700ft long and is interrupted by two transepts. These are the main departure Platforms 1 and 2, as seen from the 'Lawn' – the circulation area at the head of the platforms. The designs on the wrought iron arched ribs are seen to particular effect.

Paddington's temporary station, 1850. Although described as temporary, the arrangement shown here served for some fifteen years from 4 June 1838 until the full opening of the permanent station on 29 May 1854. The canopy on the right marks the station entrance, while the goods offices are opposite. The Prince of Wales Hotel was on the south corner of Bishops Road and Eastbourne Terrace. Queen Victoria arrived here after her first railway journey in 1842.

The Eastbourne Terrace side of the station, c.1900, featuring, from left to right: the main booking office building, a slightly taller block of railway offices and the side of the Great Western Hotel. The ornately decorated ends of the train-shed are visible through a gap in the façade which had since been filled.

Great Western Hotel, *c.*1904. Opened on 9 June 1854, the building was designed by Philip Charles Hardwick. It is in the style of a French *château*, but also has conventional classical decoration. The sculpture was by John Thomas who, like Hardwick, also worked on the Great Hall at Euston. The exterior was altered between 1936 and 1938, when a GWR monogram replaced the gross sculpted figures over the main entrance.

Frith's painting *The Railway Station*, perhaps the most famous Victorian railway painting. William Powell Frith finished *The Railway Station* in 1862. Various groups are cast about for dramatic or humourous effect, each with a story to tell. For instance, to the right a criminal is arrested, while boarding the next carriage is a bridal party. The huge canvas is now at the Royal Holloway College.

Royal Waiting Room, c.1904. Every railway of any size had special facilities for royalty, ranging from a private waiting room to an entirely separate station. The Great Western was Queen Victoria's preferred method of transport from London to Windsor and luxurious facilities were provided at both locations. The walls of this room were enamelled in salmon, with grey silk panels and had gilt mouldings.

The funeral of Edward VII, 20 May 1910. King Edward VII died on 6 May in Buckingham Palace. After lying in state in Westminster Hall, his body was taken to Windsor for burial. In this view his funeral cortège is seen proceeding down the ramp from Praed Street. This was the traditional route for departed sovereigns. Queen Victoria, George V and George VI all came this way.

Marylebone

Having spent all its money getting to London, the Great Central Railway had none left to build what should have been its biggest and best station. Instead a small and insignificant building was built with a frontage of red brick and terracotta resembling 'a branch library in a Manchester suburb' (Betjeman) and platform roofing more suited to a goods shed. The station is completely dominated by the Hotel Great Central, a far nobler edifice.

Concourse, c.1910. Wide, spacious and grossly underused: crowds came but once in a blue moon to this the last of the London termini. Typically, the first public train left on 15 March 1899 with a mere four passengers. The London extension of the Great Central was closed in 1966 and Marylebone ceased to be a regular main line station though it remains in use for suburban trains. The foliage makes a strange contrast to the harsh metal roofing.

MARYLEBONE STATION, LONDON. G.C.R.   Copyright.

The platforms, c.1905. The interior of Marylebone was the competent but hardly inspired product of Sir Douglas and Francis Fox. By 1900, the era of the great arched train-sheds was over in Britain; however, in Germany this period saw their most widespread use. The lack of action on Platform 1 and the cab road is characteristic. Father Ronald Knox declared this to be 'the only London terminus where one can hear bird song'.

Hotel Great Central, c.1905. Although not owned or built by the GCR, this was clearly a railway hotel and, with 700 beds, it was the largest in London. The architect was Colonel Robert William Edis. Beyond can be seen a glimpse of the station exterior (designed by H.W. Braddock). Opened on 1 July 1899, the hotel was converted to offices for British Railways in 1948 but is now once again a luxury hotel.

Euston

Euston (ref: J 19) opened on 20 July 1837 as terminus of the London and Birmingham Railway, the first trunk railway to reach London. The station soon became the headquarters of the LNWR, Britain's biggest and most profitable railway company. The station's traffic had long out-grown the buildings, so in 1939 the first steps to reconstruction were taken. Unfortunately, this was not carried out due to the Second World War and the sprawling mess lingered on into the 1960s.

Approach to the station from Euston Road, 1870. In response to the opening of St Pancras, the LNWR revamped Euston. These two storey lodges were added to flank the new approach road to the station. Designed by J.B. Stansby, lettering on the quoin stones records the destinations to be reached from Euston. At the same time the station name was incised on the arch. This splendid vista was available for little more than a decade before being spoiled by additions to the hotel.

The front of Euston Hotel, c.1938. This loathsome appendage, the 1881 frontage of the Hotel designed by J. McLaren, was responsible for the blocking of the view on the page opposite (the Doric Arch can just be seen through the cab entrance). Thankfully, this true Victorian monstrosity was swept away in 1963. Unfortunately, the grim, grey skyscrapers and windswept concrete are equally unappealing.

The rear of Euston Hotel, c.1905. Two matching hotels in front of the arch called the Euston and the Victoria were opened in late 1839. These were the first railway-owned hotels in the world. They were united in 1881 as the Euston Hotel with the central addition seen above. This is the side facing the arch with the original buildings, designed by Philip Hardwick, to either side.

Euston Station, London.

The Arch, *c.*1905. *C'est magnifique, mais ce n'est pas la Gare!* The focal point of old Euston was the grey granite arch (properly a Propylaeum). Designed by Philip Hardwick (senior) and completed in May 1838, the arch cost about £30,000. Also shown are two of the three then surviving lodges. The arch was unceremoniously demolished in 1961. Imagine if the Berliners had allowed the comparable Brandenburger Tor to be treated that way.

The Courtyard, *c.*1905. The arch led through into a courtyard. The ramshackle air of the place at this time (due to unplanned extensions) can be glimpsed in this view. To the right is part of the original 1837 station fabric, while in the centre is the exterior of the Great Hall. In the 1960s the site was cleared and a new station, modern and functional but soulless was erected in its place.

The Great Hall, c.1904, the grandest railway waiting room in Britain, was opened on 27 May 1849. It was designed by P.C. Hardwick, son of the architect of the arch. The cost was £150,000, more than for the whole of Kings Cross. Many of the materials used were of poor quality – the 'marble' columns being plaster. The only visible reminder of this impressive room is George Stephenson's statue by E.H. Bailey, which now languishes outside in the rain.

Enquiry office, 6 November 1929. One T.J. Tarbox is seen here in the local line enquiry office shortly before his retirement. Mr Tarbox was a typical old-time 'railway servant', having been with the company for forty-eight years. This tiny cramped room is a great contrast to the vast enquiry and ticket office of today.

Platforms 1 and 2 (c.1905) were used mainly for arrivals, with the cab road to the left. These were additions of 1873. This dull and rather murky interior is a contrast both to the architectural features of Euston (the Arch and the Hall) and to the glorious train-sheds of St Pancras and Paddington.

Approaches, c.1922. The train on the left, an early EMU (Electric Multiple Unit) of Oerlikon stock, used on the slow services to Watford, is standing on Platform 4. The other train in the view is on Platform 6. The photograph was taken by a French railway enthusiast from the end of Platform 3.

LNWR war memorial, 21 October 1921. The last addition to old Euston is the only major feature to survive the station's transformation. The memorial to the staff who died in the Great War, was designed by Robert Wynn Owen and is shown here on the day it was unveiled by Douglas Haig. The white limestone obelisk, located behind the two Euston Road lodges, stands on a granite base, bronze statues represent the four services: artillery, infantry, navy and air force.

Kings Cross and St. Pancras

St Pancras and Kings Cross (ref: I 20) are an odd pair, two more dissimilar buildings juxtapositioned it would be difficult to find. Kings Cross, headquarters of the Great Northern Railway, is no-nonsense, utilitarian brick with a few decorative features thrown in to please the public. The Midland terminus, St Pancras, is a fussy gothic monster, reputedly mistaken for a church by the stranger. In many ways the two buildings reflect the character of the people served by the respective railways: Kings Cross the phlegmatic Yorkshireman who knows the value of money; St Pancras, the Midlander with new found wealth, wanting to make his mark. Yet both are archetypal Victorian buildings.

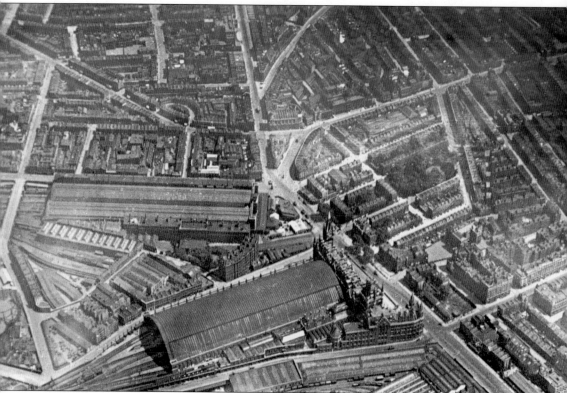

An aerial view, c.1925. Kings Cross is the central feature but the pointed gothic spires of St Pancras can also be seen. Beneath St Pancras, can be seen part of the extensive Somers Town goods depot. This is now the site of the new British Library. Between Kings Cross and St Pancras can just be made out the gentle curve of the Great Northern Hotel and the ridge and furrow roof of Kings Cross suburban station.

Midland Railway, St. Pancras Station.

St Pancras, platforms, c.1905. The interior of St Pancras is as stupendous as the outside. William Barlow was responsible for the train-shed, which was ready for the opening of the station on 1 October 1868. With its span of 245ft and height of 100ft, it was the biggest in the world. The pointed arch shape was to reduce wind resistance but contributes to the gothic feel of the station. The cab road is to the right and Platform 5 to the left.

Kings Cross, platforms, c.1910. This is the former No.1 arrival platform, now Platform 1, in the eastern of the pair of semi-circular arched halls. The ribs of the roof were originally made of laminated wood but these showed signs of strain and had to be rebuilt in iron.

Named after a short-lived monument to King George IV, Kings Cross Station opened on 14 October 1852 (this picture was taken around 1910). Lewis Cubbitt designed the building, which is basically utilitarian brick with a few architectural features – such as the fashionably Italianate turret and the Venetian windows on the office building on the left – thrown in as crowd pleasers. In front is the 'Indian Village' which was swept away in 1968.

Kings Cross, Great Northern Hotel, c.1905. The Great Northern Hotel was opened in Easter 1854 and, like the station, was designed by Lewis Cubbitt. In Italianate style, the most notable feature is the curved plan – required to fit into the curve of Pancras Road. The road was later diverted, leaving a messy space to the rear. The cost of the hotel was around £20,000. The Great Northern Hotel is the oldest surviving railway hotel but its future is uncertain.

St Pancras, Midland Grand Hotel, *c.*1950. The famous gothic St Pancras Station is really the Midland Grand Hotel, which fronts the station. London's finest railway building, it is also one of the greatest works of Sir George Gilbert Scott. The hotel admitted its first guests on 5 May 1873 but was not completed until 1876. 'London's most comfortable hotel' closed in 1935 and was in use as offices at this time. The open taxi is straight out of 'The Ladykillers'.

Liverpool Street and Broad Street

Unlike the grand pairing of Kings Cross and St Pancras, Liverpool Street and Broad Street (ref: K 23) are a more prosaic pair. Liverpool Street, former headquarters of the Great Eastern, is the principal entry to London from East Anglia. The busiest station in Britain, old Liverpool Street consisted of three elements: the original west side of 1874 with its spectacular train-shed, the less interesting east side, dating from 1892, flanking Bishopsgate and the Great Eastern Hotel. Broad Street, City terminus of the North London Railway (see section 2), was robust and compact, but alas ailing in recent years. The couple has been split by the demise of the elder partner.

INTERIOR, LIVERPOOL STREET STATION, LONDON.   209801.J.V.

Liverpool Street, *c.1925*. The lively scene, focusing on the concourse to Platforms 5 to 8, mixes the bustle of the life of a station with a hint of the gothic wonders of the train-shed. The slender piers spring up from nowhere and appear too fragile to support the weighty spandrels above. This is the original (western) part of the station, designed by Edward Wilson, and dating from 1875. Thankfully, it was saved during the recent rebuilding.

Liverpool Street, c.1910. This is the gothic style exterior of the west side which dates from when the station opened on 2 February 1874. The architect was Edward Wilson. The suburban booking office, to the left of the clock tower, was added in 1883. Everything seen here was pulled down when the station was rebuilt between 1987 and 1991. The current buildings on the site are in the same style and incorporate some original decoration.

Liverpool Street, unexecuted design, 1864. This is what Liverpool Street could have looked like. This design by one Robert Sinclair for the proposed station is dated 1864. In the event the new Great Eastern terminus was built at a low level to allow through running with the Metropolitan. This did not last more than a few years but left an indelible impression on the layout of the station.

The Great Eastern Hotel – seen here in 1906 – opened for business in 1884. The building, in the Dutch Renaissance style, was designed by Charles Edward Barry, son of the Houses of Parliament architect and a relative of the Barry who worked on the Cannon Street and Charing Cross hotels. An extension was added in 1900-1901. The architect was then Robert William Edis, but the style is identical.

Hamilton Hall, Great Eastern Hotel, c.1905. Lord Claud Hamilton was the chairman of the Great Eastern between 1893 and 1923. A name change to the Liverpool Street Hotel was considered at this time, but this title was never officially adopted. This fine hall dates from the extension of 1900-1901.

Broad Street, c.1905. William Baker, the company's engineer, designed this very Victorian station which opened on 1 November 1865. The hideous iron footbridge in front, leading directly to the concourse from the street, was added in 1890. The arcaded staircase on the side did the same job with more grace. At the time of this view the station was at its peak but subsequently usage shrank until it was just a shabby hulk and it was closed on 30 June 1986.

Approaches, c.1910. This view shows the vast extent of railway activity around Broad Street. Signal box Broad Street No.1 stands by a coaling stage and water towers. As well as serving nine platforms, tracks also led to extensive goods yards. This area has been completely transformed after the station's demolition in 1985-1986 and the jaunty Broadgate office complex has been erected on its site.

London's City Stations

Around the City of London, in tight formation, are arrayed the stations which every weekday morning disgorge workers fresh from their homes in 'commuterland', and every weekday evening are the centre of their great rush home again. In Edwardian times there were seven of these stations: Broad Street, Liverpool Street, Fenchurch Street, London Bridge, Cannon Street, Blackfriars and Holborn Viaduct.

Cannon Street (ref: L 22), 1867. A typical street scene in the City has the SER's City Terminus Hotel as the background. The frontage of Cannon Street, which opened on 1 September 1866, is akin to Charing Cross, as the architect E. M. Barry designed both. The hotel was closed and became offices in 1931. On 11 May 1941 the station suffered severe damage as the result of bombing. Patched up, the ex-hotel, known as Southern House, soldiered on it was rebuilt in 1963.

165   LONDON. — *London Bridge Station.* — LL.

London Bridge (ref: M 23), *c*.1910. London Bridge was London's first terminus. Opened as the end of a short local line to Greenwich on 10 October 1836, the station was soon divided into SER (later SECR) and LBSCR parts. This is the LBSCR frontage designed by David Mocatta and dating from 1854. On the right is the former station hotel by Henry Currey erected in 1861. The frontage buildings and ex-hotel were destroyed by fire on 29 December 1940.

London Bridge, aerial view, *c*.1925. In this view from the mid-1920s the station's relationship to London Bridge and the City can clearly be seen. The dividing line between the ex-LBSCR (left) and ex-SECR (right) sides is clearly evident but was shortly to disappear. The LBSCR arched train-shed flanked by ridge and furrow roofing can be distinguished from the SECR's open platforms.

Blackfriars (not shown on map), from the river, c.1950. The view of St Paul's Cathedral from Blackfriars railway bridge is one of the little known railway wonders of London. The pitched roof of the station's train-shed can be seen directly below the dome of St Pauls. Opened on 10 May 1886 by the London, Chatham & Dover Railway, the station was called St Paul's until 1937.

Holborn Viaduct (ref: K 21), c.1905. Opened on 2 March 1874, Holborn Viaduct was the LCDR's main City terminus. The frontage included a railway-owned hotel designed by Lewis J. Isaacs. The hotel closed in 1917 and was used as offices until destroyed by fire during an air raid on 10-11 May 1941. An office block was erected as a replacement in 1963. Holborn Viaduct Station closed in 1990 being replaced by City Thameslink on almost the same site.

Fenchurch Street (ref: L 23), concourse facing east, c.1910. Opened on 2 August 1841 as the London end of a short line to Blackwall, the station was totally rebuilt in 1852-1853 to the design of George Berkeley. Although owned by the Great Eastern, the station's traffic came mainly from the London, Tilbury & Southend Railway. The destination board is misleading; trains went from here to North Greenwich (really the Isle of Dogs), North Woolwich and Tilbury with Gravesend accessible by ferry.

Fenchurch Street, concourse facing west, c.1910. The refreshment rooms and the telegraph office which it backed onto, as well as the gates and bookstall seen in the above view, dated from 1883 to 1885 and were cleared away between 1932 and 1935. The arched roof seen here was pulled down and replaced by an office development over the platforms in the early 1990s.

Waterloo

Waterloo (ref: M 20) is the largest station in Britain, with more than twenty platforms, and one of the busiest. Formerly terminus and headquarters of the London & South Western Railway, it serves the South West including the busy ports of Plymouth, Portsmouth and Southampton, as well as having an extensive suburban network. Waterloo is currently the terminus for Channel Tunnel trains. Technically the station should be called Lambeth but this had unwanted slummy connotations. Thus Waterloo is named after the nearby bridge (rather than directly after the battle as is often presumed).

Waterloo Station. London & South Western Railwa

Platforms, September 1910. Waterloo, like Euston, had grown up haphazardly after its opening on 11 July 1848. By 1900, rebuilding was essential. Reconstruction started from the east of the station and, by 1910, had reached the situation shown here. The new Platforms 1 to 5, with their spacious new roofing, are already in use. To the right the original cab yard can just be seen under the remaining part of the low canopies of the old South Station.

War memorial, 1922. The Victory Arch forms the pedestrian entrance to the station from York Road but also doubles up as the memorial to the staff of the London & South Western Railway who died in the First World War. The architect was James Robb Scott. Sadly, it is placed in a particularly cramped position which makes it difficult to fully appreciate this grandiose gesture. The crowd dates from the unveiling on 21 March 1922 but has been superimposed on a later picture of the arch.

Waterloo, c.1920. An army of porters waits under the covered cab road outside the main booking office. This part of the façade runs parallel to Waterloo Road and fronts the main booking office, which opened on 11 June 1911. Around the corner, building work is still in progress. Underneath the 'drive slowly' sign the viaduct leading to Charing Cross Station can just be made out.

Charing Cross

Charing Cross (ref: L 20), the West End terminus of the South Eastern (later South Eastern & Chatham) Railway, has survived numerous attempts to close it, as well as the collapse of the arched roof of the train-shed and severe damage in the Second World War. Once the main station for continental traffic, today it caters almost exclusively for commuter traffic. Located in the heart of the West End, within sight of Trafalgar Square, it is one of the most prominent of London's termini.

The station (seen here around 1910) opened on 11 January 1864 and the railway owned hotel above on 15 May 1865. Edward Middleton Barry designed the street frontage. The name comes from the Eleanor Cross, which stood nearby from 1294 to 1647. The monument visible in the forecourt is Barry's reproduction dating from 1863. The hotel roof was badly damaged in the air raid on 17 April 1941 and has been rebuilt in a timid modern style.

Charing Cross disaster, 5 December 1905. Sir John Hawkshaw's arched roof was undergoing routine maintenance on 5 December 1905 when, at 3.57 p.m., 70ft of the roof crashed down. Three unfortunate workmen reconstructing the Avenue Theatre (left foreground) died as well as three people in the station. The collapse was blamed on a flaw in the welding which had been disturbed. The station was closed until March while the roof was replaced.

Approaches, c.1910. The 1906 replacement roof was a simple ridge and furrow affair. Utilitarian and dull, it was surmounted by the crest of the South Eastern & Chatham at the country end. The crest was replaced by that of the Southern Railway in the 1920s. In the early 1990s the space above the platforms was built on and a 'post-modern' edifice occupies the space today.

Victoria

Victoria (ref: N 18) is the London station most familiar to Europeans as most continental traffic departs from here. Prior to Grouping, Victoria was effectively divided into two separate stations belonging to the London, Brighton & South Coast (or Brighton side) and the South Eastern & Chatham (Chatham side). In Edwardian times, the frontages of both were rebuilt in baroque style. The architectural competition between the two companies for the most stylish station building resulted in 'London's most conspicuous monument to commercial rivalry' (Betjeman). After 1923 the walls between the two sides of the station came down, but the distinctions in architecture remain.

Chatham side, c.1915. This is the continental (long distance) platform, formerly the main departure platform, with the original station building to the left. In this structure, which faces Hudson's Place, were the main booking offices, waiting rooms and the Royal Waiting Room. This type of W.H. Smith bookstall was known as a dreadnought!

Chatham side before rebuilding, c.1905. This is virtually how the station looked when it opened on 25 August 1862 as the West End terminus of the London, Chatham & Dover Railway. The main buildings were around the corner in Hudson's Place. The two great arches of the train-shed designed by Henry Fowler survived the rebuilding.

Chatham side after rebuilding, c.1910. By 1908 the ramshackle buildings had given way to this splendid frontage carried out in the grandiose baroque style favoured in Edwardian times. The architect was Alfred W. Blomfeld, while Henry C. Fehr provided the statuary. The Great Western had a prominent display but few services terminated here.

Grosvenor Hotel, c.1905. The hotel was attached to the LBSCR half of Victoria Station. Dating from 1861, it was designed by J.T. Knowles. The building is a typical mid-Victorian pile with interesting (if impractical) decoration. Inset roundels feature portraits of famous contemporaries.

Brighton side, c.1915. Behind the bookstall can be seen the wires of the overhead electric trains, which ran to many suburban destinations from 1909. Trains from Victoria last used overhead wires in 1929 when conversion to third rail pick-up was completed. The post office dated from the rebuilding of 1908 and closed in 1967.

Brighton side before rebuilding, c.1905. The Brighton side was opened on 1 October 1860. These are the unattractive station buildings before reconstruction. The Porte Cochérè dated from 1880 and, after the station was rebuilt, was taken away to Hove, near Brighton, and reused. There is not an internal combustion engine to be seen.

Brighton side after rebuilding, c.1915. The rebuilding of the station was completed in 1908. The architect of this baroque edifice, whose upper storeys were an annexe to the Grosvenor, was Charles L. Morgan. Underneath the awning, a sign advertises the Elevated Electric – an early electrification project of the LBSCR. In the space of a few years horse cabs and buses have given way to petrol driven ones.

Royal train, Brighton side, 1906. The multitude of crests and crowns make it obvious whose train this is. 4-4-0 No.42 *His Majesty* prepares to depart on King Edward VII's visit to Epsom Downs for the Derby Day Races. The King was a great patron of the Brighton since it served several of his favourite racecourses. The sumptuous LBSCR royal train was built for him in 1897 and the carriages were polished mahogany with gold lining. After Grouping, this royal train was downgraded to first class use. A Charlie Chaplin look-a-like, to the left, has been hard at work whitewashing the coal.

Two

North London Railway

Opened in 1850-1851, the North London Railway was conceived by the LNWR as a long goods siding to the docks. However, passenger services developed rapidly and in 1865 'the Happy Afterthought' to Broad Street opened. Thereafter the NLR was effectively three sections: the City extension, the Western (Dalston to Chalk Farm) and the Eastern (Dalston to Poplar). In 1909 the LNWR took over management of the line. The western arm was electrified in 1916, while the eastern half declined and closed to passengers in 1944. Proposals to close the line completely, in the 1960s, were rejected, but the 1865 City line was closed in 1986. The railway has undergone a renaissance in recent years with the reopening of part of the eastern route. The present North London Line runs from Richmond to North Woolwich.

Two other lines have always been associated with the North London: the Hampstead Junction Railway, from Willesden Junction to Camden Town, and the Victoria Park Branch of the Great Eastern. Along with the GER's North Woolwich branch and parts of two other railways, both are now part of the North London Line.

Hackney Station, 1851 (ref: G 25). It was not only the Underground which spurred on the growth of suburbia. Half a century earlier the North London had been built through open countryside on the outskirts of the metropolis. Within the space of twenty years, almost the whole line was a dense mass of terraced houses interspersed by the spires of Victorian gothic churches.

Dalston Western Junction, c.1910 (ref: G 24). A Broad Street-bound train passes from the original 1850 line, between Camden and the docks, to the City extension. The signal box still exists although it has not been used for some time. The townscape depicted here is typical of that through which the North London still runs.

46

Chalk Farm Station, *c*.1910 (ref: H 17). There had been a station in this vicinity since 1851 but this building dated from 1871. It seems not to have been completed – the panels over the entrance should have carried the station and company names. The station was renamed Primrose Hill in 1950 and, subsequently, the building was extensively altered. Primrose Hill closed on 28 September 1992.

Camden Town Station, *c*.1905 (ref: H 18). The first Camden Station of 1850 stood some way off in St Pancras Way. Like most of the stations on the route, Camden received a new building designed by Edwin Henry Horne that opened on 3 December 1870. It is typical of his work and is the only one to survive in railway use. The journey time to the City is as fast, if not faster, than the tube today.

Canonbury Station, c.1905 (ref: G 22). Opened on 1 September 1858 as Newington Road and Balls Pond, it was resited and renamed Canonbury in 1870. The building dated from that time and is an exact duplicate of that at Barnsbury. At Canonbury, in common with many of the larger NLR stations, the upper floor was later used as a billiards hall. The stationmaster's house, seen to the right, still survives.

Caledonian Road and Barnsbury Station, c.1906 (ref: H 21). Barnsbury opened on 21 November 1870 as a replacement for an earlier station in Caledonian Road. There were two exits – to Roman Road and to Caledonian Road. This picture shows the view towards those at the western or Caledonian Road end.

HIGHBURY STATION.

Highbury & Islington Station, *c.*1905 (ref: G 21). Opened on 29 September 1850, this station was rebuilt to the form shown here in 1872. The building, in Italian gothic style, is naturally the work of E.H. Horne and incorporates a block of shops and the Cock Tavern. During the Second World War the street level building was badly damaged by bombing requiring it to be rebuilt in the 1950s and 1960s.

Highbury & Islington Station, *c.*1906 (ref: G 21). The platforms at this time were gas lit and bedecked with advertisements. The station, popularly always known as plain Highbury, is now a major interchange between the North London and the Victoria and Great Northern City tube routes.

Mildmay Park Station, *c.*1907 (ref: G 23). One of the last additions to the line and opened on 1 January 1880, this station was also one of the first to close on 1 October 1934. The small but attractive booking office building was probably the work of Horne and was finally demolished in 1987.

Mildmay Park Station, *c.*1907 (ref: G 23). The platforms vanished not long after the station closed. A most dramatic event occurred here on 9 January 1914 when young William Starchfield was found strangled under a carriage seat when a train pulled into the station. His father was tried but acquitted of the murder. The case remains unsolved.

Dalston Junction Station, *c.*1904 (ref: G 24). Located on the new line to Broad Street, this station opened on 1 November 1865, replacing nearby Kingsland (the site of which was used for a new station in 1983). The booking office building stood on the south side of Dalston Lane and was demolished in 1970. The station closed on 30 June 1986.

Dalston Junction Station, *c.*1905 (ref: G 24). A train for Broad Street arrives at Platform 4, while bulkily dressed Edwardian ladies await trains at Platforms 2 and 3. An impressive affair at this time, with six platforms and extensive buildings, scarcely a trace remains in the area today.

Hackney Station, Mare Street.

Hackney Station, c.1905 (ref: G 25). Originally opened in 1850, the building seen here was used from 1 December 1870. The station closed on 15 May 1944 but happily reopened on 12 May 1980 as Hackney Central. The old street level building, showing the characteristic Moorish horseshoe arches, is the work of Horne and still survives, although is now in commercial use. Sadly, the large front porch has recently been demolished.

Church Road, Homerton.

Homerton Station, c.1906 (ref: G 26). Opened 1 October 1868, the station closed in 1944 and reopened in 1985 with an entrance on the other side of the bridge. The platform buildings and signal box have vanished and only a small fragment of the cavernous street building remains today.

Bow Station, *c*.1904 (ref: J 28). Opened on 26 September 1850, the station was rebuilt in 1870 to a design by Horne that incorporated a massive concert hall called the Bromley & Bow Institute. To the right is the Match Tax Testimonial Drinking Fountain, now sadly demolished. Closed on 15 May 1944, the buildings lingered until 1975. The new Docklands Light Railway Bow Station is located opposite.

Poplar Station, *c*.1910 (ref: L 29). Poplar East India Dock Road, opened on 1 August 1866, was the terminus of the passenger trains from Broad Street, although the tracks continued into the docks. The neat, if undistinguished, building was irreparably damaged by a flying bomb on 16 June 1944 but the station had closed the month before. All Saints Station on the Docklands Light Railway stands on the site.

Victoria Park Junction, c.1905 (ref: G 27). At Victoria Park the Great Eastern Railway branch to Stratford, opened on 15 August 1854, diverged from the original North London line to Poplar. The signal box was rebuilt in 1961. This location ceased to be a junction in 1984 when the old route to the docks, which was still in occasional use for goods, was totally shut.

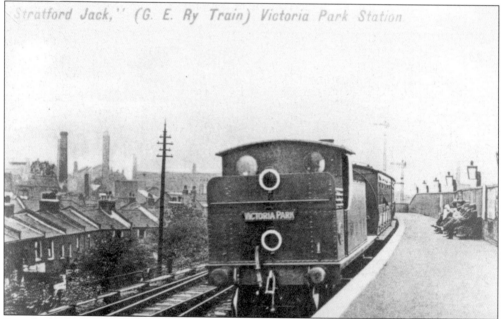

Stratford train at Victoria Park Station, c.1905 (ref: G 27). From 1866 to 1942 a shuttle service operated from Victoria Park to Stratford. The Great Eastern engines, which pulled the trains, were for some reason known as 'Stratford Jacks'. Passenger services were revived on this line in 1980 and it now forms part of the through route to North Woolwich.

Finchley Road & Frognal Station, *c.*1903 (ref: G 15). The Hampstead Junction Railway was built by an independent company but was absorbed into the LNWR not long after it opened on 2 January 1860. This was one of the original stations. The low undistinguished buildings are typical of those on the line and survived until the late 1960s. The tiled arch on the left led to a depot of the Aylesbury Dairy Company.

Kensal Rise Station, *c.*1907 (ref: I 12). This station, known as Kensal Green until 1890, opened on 1 July 1873 replacing an earlier version that was too close to Willesden Junction. The structure shown here dates to around 1893 and was demolished for road widening in 1968. The HJR was always almost exclusively served by NLR trains and now forms an integral part of the current North London Line.

North London train at Enfield Station, c.1900 (not on map). 4-4-0T No.19 heads a train for Broad Street at the Great Northern Station. The NLR ran services to Potters Bar, Enfield, Alexandra Palace and High Barnet, via the Canonbury to Finsbury Park link. This was opened for passengers on 18 January 1875 and continued in use until 1976. The guards compartment with its clerestory roof was a feature of NLR rolling stock.

North London locomotive, c.1930. The North London built its own locomotives at its Bow Works. The majority were variations of the type shown here. 4-4-0T No.6444, seen here in LMS days, is a typical example. The NLR's home-produced engines were largely withdrawn before the Second World War.

Three

Metropolitan
and District

The original section of the Metropolitan Railway opened on 10 January 1863 and ran in cuttings and shallow tunnels from Paddington to Farringdon Street. This later formed the northern part of the Inner Circle, now the Circle Line, which was completed in 1884. Within thirty years, the 'Met', as it was affectionately known, had expanded into and beyond London's northwestern suburbs. This 'Extension Line' made the company into a 'main line in miniature'. Both the Circle and the Inner suburban extension line underwent Electrification in 1905. The Metropolitan survived Grouping only to be amalgamated with the Underground group in 1933 to form London Transport.

Jointly owned by the Metropolitan and Great Western, the Hammersmith & City ran from Paddington to Hammersmith.

The District Railway, officially the Metropolitan District Railway, was promoted to close the southern side of the Circle and later spread into the western suburbs. Electrified in the early 1900s, many of its stations were reconstructed by the District's architect H.W. Ford.

Building of the Metropolitan Railway at Kings Cross, 1861 (ref: I 20). The tunnels on the Inner Circle were built by the so-called cut-and-cover method, which caused enormous disruption. Euston Road curves off to the left – the tall block of houses was later pulled down for St Pancras. Kings Cross seems unfamiliar without the clutter of the 'Indian village'. The building with the steeply pitched roof is the Great Northern Hotel.

Portland Road Station, *c.*1905 (ref: J 18). This building occupies an island site and was originally surmounted by two domes. The Italianate architecture on the original stretch of the Metropolitan Railway was probably the work of Sir John Fowler (the engineer of the line) and J.H. Stevens. The station has been Great Portland Street since 1917 and was rebuilt in 1930.

Baker Street Station, *c.*1905 (ref: J 17). At first just another stop on the original 1863 line, Baker Street became a junction early on with the opening of a branch to Swiss Cottage. However, it did not become really important until the expansion of the 'Met' to the north west of London and beyond in the 1880s and 1890s. From 1911 to 1930 the station was rebuilt to a form that would dwarf the paltry buildings shown here.

Moorgate Street Station, *c.*1918 (ref: K 22). What was in practice the Met's City terminus opened on 23 December 1865. It was rebuilt between 1895 and 1903, the architect being George Campbell Sherrin. The station building was in two halves: one for the use of the Metropolitan (nearest) and one for SECR, Midland and GNR suburban trains.

Bomb damage at Moorgate Station, *c.*1941 (ref: K 22). Following the air raid on the night of 29 December 1940, fires raged out of control in many parts of the City of London. This was the 'Second Great Fire of London'. Moorgate Station was totally destroyed – this was the booking office. The station was rebuilt in 1965.

Farringdon & High Holborn Station at night, c.1930 (ref: K 21). In the 1920s most of the original Metropolitan stations were rebuilt to designs by C.W. Clarke, the Met's chief architect. With its white-glazed moulded tiles, this example, dating from 1922, is typical. At the same time, the name was lengthened – the fact that the station is some distance from High Holborn was ignored! The building still exists but the station is now plain Farringdon. The Metropolitan adopted the diamond as their logo (as seen on the porch) to distinguish itself from the Underground with its famous circle and bar motif.

SWISS COTTAGE. Station.

Swiss Cottage Station, *c.*1903 (ref: H 15). Located on the corner of Swiss Terrace and Finchley Road, this building was similar to contemporary stations on the District, such as Bayswater, which survives today. Opened on 13 April 1868, it was the terminus of a single line branch from Baker Street until 1879. The exterior was rebuilt in 1929. The station closed on 17 August 1940 and was replaced by one on the Bakerloo (now on the Jubilee) Line.

Finchley Road Station, *c.*1910 (ref: G 15). Finchley Road opened on 30 June 1879 at the start of the Met's leap to the north west. This was the original building, which was replaced in 1913-1914. The block of shops behind the station survives today.

Willesden Green Station, *c.*1910 (ref: G 11). This building is characteristic of the style of architecture used on the Extension line. The massive moulded chimneys and half-timbering mark it as an example of the Domestic Revival style. The architect was A. McDermott. Dating from the station's opening on 20 November 1879, this building lasted until 1925. Today only Jubilee Line trains run to and from Willesden Green.

Kingsbury-Neasden Station, *c.*1905 (ref: F 9). This charming building, unlike its close relative at Willesden Green, survives today. The station, opened on 2 August 1880, has been through several name changes and is now simply Neasden. Like Willesden Green, it is now served only by Jubilee line trains. Neasden was the Met's railway town – like Crewe for the LNWR or the GWR's Swindon.

NEASDEN POWER STATION.

Neasden power station, 1905 (ref: F 9). This bulky edifice was built between 1903 and 1905 for the Baker Street to Uxbridge electrification. The architect was Matthew Garbutt. It was closed and demolished in 1968. In the background at the extreme right can be seen 'Watkin's Folly'. This was a tower intended to rival Eiffel's and was built in 1890-1891 on Wembley Hill. Only the first stage was reached before the money ran out. It was taken down in 1907.

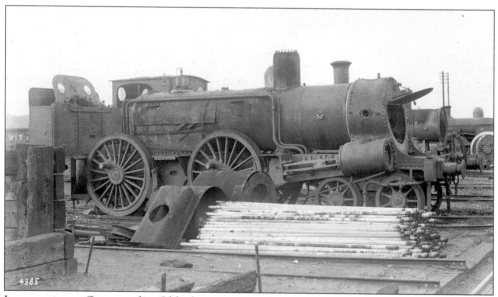

Locomotives Graveyard! Old locomotives being scrapped at Neasden, c.1908. Electrification rendered a large number of locomotives and rolling stock redundant. Being specially designed for working the enclosed Inner Circle, there was little chance of resale. This is the remains of one of the 4-4-0 tanks later known as 'A' class.

Steam and electric on the Circle, near Edgware Road, 1905 (ref: K 16). To the left, an early Metropolitan engine heads bunker first towards Hammersmith. On the right, an early electric Circle train stands in a siding by the 1863 loco shed. Electric traction replaced steam on this part of the Circle in September 1905. In the distance to the right is the grandiose pile of the Hotel Great Central (see page 17).

Early electric train on the Inner Circle, *c.*1906. The impressive arched train hall, wooden platforms, suspended gaslights and plentiful advertisements were typical of stations on the Circle. This is one on the western half of the circle. The first electric trains used on the Circle were built in 1904-1905 and lasted until the late 1930s.

Metropolitan Extension Line train, *c.*1927. Later known as T Stock, these trains were delivered in 1927. Built for use on the electric services to Watford and Rickmansworth, which commenced in 1925, this type was scrapped in the early 1960s.

Royal Oak Station, c.1903 (ref: K 14). Although the Hammersmith & City was officially a joint line, it was dominated by the Great Western. This is the original brick booking office building, dating from when the station opened on 30 October 1871. With its French pavilion style roof and decorative foundry work cresting, it is typical of GWR work (see also Ealing Broadway, page 102). It was rebuilt in 1904.

Hammersmith Station, c.1910 (ref: N 11). The terminus of the line opened on 1 December 1868. The building shown here was built in 1907-1909 to the design of the GWR architect P.E. Culverhouse and the GWR engineers department. Today the station frontage merely lacks the canopy.

Walham Green Station, c.1905 (ref: P 14). The earliest stations of the District were identical in style to those on the Circle section of the Metropolitan reflecting the District's offshoot status. After independence the poverty stricken District expanded into the southwestern suburbs. Walham Green, now Fulham Broadway, opened on 1 March 1880, is typical: cheaply built and unattractive with large hoardings. This station was rebuilt in 1910.

Turnham Green Station, c.1914 (ref: N 18). Between Hammersmith and Chiswick Park the District took advantage of the existing LSWR Richmond to Kensington line. Stations were owned by the South Western, which ran trains on the route from 1 January 1869 until 1916. The District service began on 1 June 1877 and still continues. The booking office building, a single storey version of Gunnersbury (see page 107), still exists.

Southfields Station, c.1915 (not on map). The Putney Bridge to Wimbledon line of the District was similar in status to the section containing Turnham Green, mentioned on the opposite page. On 3 June 1889 the station was first used by District trains – before those of the owning company. The LSWR ran trains over this line from 1889 to 1940. The yellow and red brick pavilion station building was altered around 1905 and still exists today.

Hammersmith Station, c.1920 (ref: O 11). Hammersmith District Station opened on 9 September 1874 and was rebuilt for the arrival of Piccadilly tube trains in 1906. The building shown here was carried out in dull purple tiles and was probably the work of H.W. Ford, who was heavily influenced by Leslie Green's work on the early Underground stations. The station was thoroughly rebuilt in the early 1990s.

Earls Court Station, *c.*1910 (ref: N 14). Earls Court opened on 30 October 1871. The exterior was rebuilt in 1906 to the form shown here. This building is a close relation of Hammersmith but here the tiling is light brown with blue lettering. This example is still standing. Above the porch are two NTC (National Telephone Company) signs.

Barons Court Station, *c.*1906 (not on map). This station was opened on 9 October 1905 and was served by Piccadilly trains from 1906. The architect was H.W. Ford, who may have been assisted by others. It is a charming building of light green coloured tiling and shows a number of Art Nouveau touches – particularly the flowing lines of the corner plaque. The building still exists.

Ealing Broadway Station, *c*.1935 (ref: K 5). Opened 1 July 1879, the street level building was rebuilt to the form shown here in 1905. Constructed of white Portland stone with classical ornamentation, this station is a typical example of Ford's work. This building has not been used for railway purposes since 1966 and the entrance to the District line platforms is currently through the main line station building.

Charing Cross Station, *c*.1930 (ref: L 20). Now Embankment, this is the District-Northern-Bakerloo interchange station as rebuilt in 1914 to a design by H.W. Ford. The station had been in use since 30 May 1870. Identical facades face Villiers Street (this one) and the Embankment itself. The shadow has been cast by the Hungerford railway bridge.

District locomotive, *c.*1884. The first Metropolitan and District locomotives were built by Beyer, Peacock & Co. of Manchester. This is a typical example of the 4-4-0 condensing tank engine later known as 'A' Class. No.42 was built in 1883 and sold on in 1906. The engines used on the District differed from those on the Metropolitan by having weatherboards bent back over the cab. The District ran to Windsor for a short period between 1883 and 1885 only.

District train, 1928. The postcard illustrating this K Class motor car was produced as part of a set commemorating the diamond jubilee of the District. The control of marker lights and the destination board from within the cab were a new feature at this time. This car was built at the Birmingham Railway Carriage & Wagon Co. works and was scrapped in the 1950s.

Four

The Tubes

The use of deep level tunnel lined with segmental iron sections (colloquially 'tube') avoided the massive disruption of cut-and-cover work. Thick underlying clay made tube construction easy. The first tube was the experimental Tower Subway, but rapid transportation deep underground had to wait until electrical traction became practicable. The City & South London Railway, the world's first underground electric railway, opened in 1890 and now forms part of the Northern Line. This railway and the Waterloo & City failed to take the public's fancy as did the Central London Railway. A flurry of schemes followed the CLR including the Great Northern & City Railway. The Bakerloo, Piccadilly and Hampstead lines, collectively known as the London Electric Railway, came next. These form the core of the modern Underground and had common architecture and rolling stock. However, the 1920s and 1930s were the 'golden years' of the Underground, when many of the central stations were rebuilt to grand designs and most lines were extended far into the suburbs.

Tube under construction, London, c.1905. One of the workers smokes the clay pipe traditional to navvies. The foreman can be recognized by his smart bowler hat. The work appears to be being carried out under compressed air – used when waterlogged ground was encountered. The principle of tube construction – iron segments bolted together – can be clearly seen. The rails are part of the contractor's narrow-gauge railway.

Entrance to Tower Subway, 1870. The originator of the tube was Peter William Barlow, engineer of the Tower Subway. This was a short tunnel between Tower Hill and Vine Street, off Tooley Street. It was formally opened on 2 August 1870. The line was reached by lifts housed in kiosks on either bank. The fare was two pence First, and one penny Second Class.

Carriage on Tower Subway, 1870. The line was cable-operated. The carriage seated fourteen passengers. The journey, about a quarter of a mile, took around a minute. Within a few months, it had been converted to a foot tunnel, which itself was closed in 1894. A commercial failure, the method of construction had been proved sound.

The Oval Station, *c.*1907. Oval was one of the original stations of the CSLR, which opened on 18 December 1890. The architect was T. Phillips Figgis. Five stations were constructed in a similar style but only Kennington remains recognizable. The larger dome housed the lift gear. Oval Station was almost completely rebuilt in 1924.

City & South London platforms, Euston, *c.*1910. To the right is one of the original C&SL electric locos. Revolutionary in their day, they were used until 1925. The carriages are typical of early tube stock, featuring the gated vestibules through which one entered and left the train. Each was attended by a gateman. The C&SL reached Euston on 12 May 1907. This is now the southbound Northern Line City branch.

Waterloo & City platforms, Waterloo, c.1898. The Waterloo & City was built by the LSWR to link its London terminus on the south bank with the City of London. The line has only two stations: Bank and Waterloo. The signal cabin is to the left. Overhead latticed bridges link the two platforms. It is easy to see why this dark drab line was known as 'the Drain'.

Waterloo & City train, 23 June 1950. Trailer car No.S85 is seen on 23 June 1950 in the sidings at Waterloo before being hoisted down to the line. The rolling stock on the W&C has only been changed twice in its history. The original cars lasted until 1940 before being replaced with the type shown here. These trains were phased out in the 1990s.

Essex Road Station, c.1905. Adverts on the windows proclaim '1d any station' and '7 minutes to Finsbury, 6 minutes to Moorgate'. Opened on 14 February 1904, the GNCR was the only tube built big enough for main line trains – originally GNR suburban trains were to have run directly to the City. Company squabbles lead to the GNCR being a self-contained shuttle for most of its life. This station has changed little.

Moorgate Street Station, 1904. The original GNCR stock seen here resembled contemporary American trains. Through the cab window is the 'dead man's handle' which must be depressed to keep the train in motion. In 1976 the line was finally linked with the Kings Cross suburban network. Shortly before the handover, this platform was the scene of a terrible train crash on 28 February 1975 when forty-three people died.

Lots Road power station, c.1906. Built for the electrification of the District and Circle Lines, in time the 'Chelsea Monster' came to supply power for the whole of the Underground and the tramways. Work began in March 1902 and the inauguration was on 1 February 1905. The crowded WLER Chelsea Basin depot is in front of the power station.

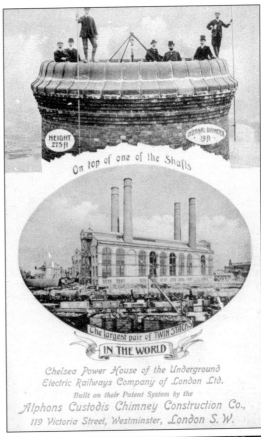

On top of one of the Shafts

HEIGHT 275 ft

INTERNAL DIAMETER 19 ft

The largest pair of TWIN STACKS

IN THE WORLD

Chelsea Power House of the Underground Electric Railways Company of London Ltd.

Built on their Patent System by the

Alphons Custodis Chimney Construction Co.,

119 Victoria Street, Westminster, London S.W.

Lots Road power station, c.1906. 'The old warm gently roaring power house with its glowing slowly moving chain grates, its glistening rows of humming generators and it's parquet floored control room all knobbly with polished dials and instruments with above the plumes of smoke drifting from its tall chimneys…' (*London's Underground*, H.F. Howson).

GREAT NORTHERN, PICCADILLY & BROMPTON Ry. POWER HOUSE, CHELSEA.

South Kensington Station

South Kensington Station, c.1909. The hoarding gives the line's full title: 'Great Northern, Piccadilly & Brompton Railway'. South Kensington opened on 8 January 1907 after the rest of the line, thus the banding is of the Hampstead pattern using black letters on white tiles to spell the station name (gold lettering was used on the other lines). The building still exists but is used for ventilation purposes. To the left is the District station.

Golders Green Station, 1907. Opened on 22 June 1907, Golders Green was the northern terminus and only open-air station on the Hampstead line. The building was unique and probably built without the aid of an architect. Behind the red brick booking office are the platforms and carriage shed. To the left the gated ends of a train of original stock may be seen. On closer inspection the tree has had the canopy built round it.

Baker Street Station, 1906. The Baker Street & Waterloo Railway (shortened to Bakerloo) opened on 10 March 1906. The LER lines had standardized street buildings designed by Leslie Green. These had two floors with a flat roof, which could be built on if required. Although functional, arts and crafts decoration was used sparingly (e.g. the wrought iron lamp brackets). This building was demolished many years ago.

Belsize Park Station, 1907. Belsize Park opened on 22 June 1907 with the rest of the Charing Cross, Euston & Hampstead Railway – or Hampstead line (now part of the Northern). The steel-framed structure was clothed with ruby red terracotta glazed blocks. Although described as pompous, ugly and unattractive, the buildings were fire proof, spacious, hard-wearing and easy to clean

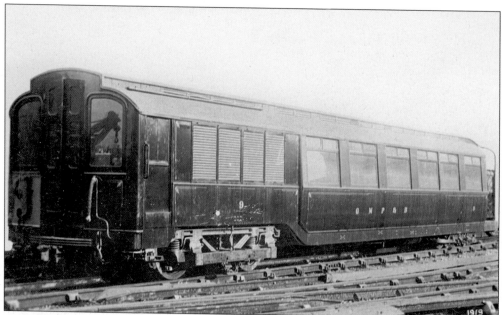

Piccadilly motor car, *c.*1906. This is a typical example of the first tube stock used on all the lines of the London Electric. The original Piccadilly rolling stock was mainly built in France and Hungary. The livery was Midland Lake (maroon).

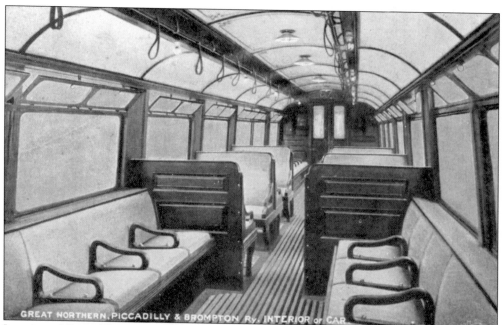

Interior of Piccadilly car, *c.*1906. The seats in the original London Electric stock were rattan covered and austere. Entry was from platforms at the ends of the cars which were protected by hand-operated lattice gates. The latter were abolished in the 1920s.

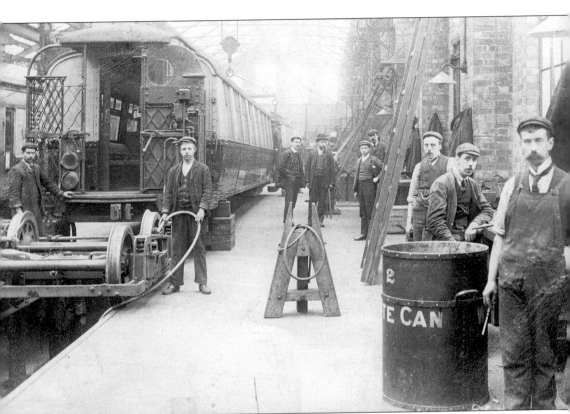

London Road depot, 1906. The workshops and maintenance buildings of the Bakerloo (at London Road), Hampstead (at Golders Green) and Piccadilly (Lillie Bridge) lines were all virtually identical. This is the lifting shop at London Road. Nearest the camera is a control trailer of the original tube stock. The workers are all doing heavy manual work in suit, collar and tie! The foreman wears a bowler, whereas ordinary workmen have flat caps.

Balham, c.1935. This building is typical of the modernistic station exteriors designed by Charles Holden for the southern extension to Morden of what is now the Northern Line. Inside stairs lead down to a booking hall beneath the roadway. Balham opened on 13 September 1926 and adjoins the main line suburban station part of which is seen to the left. To the right a tram emerges from beneath the railway bridge.

Piccadilly Circus Station, 1928. The original Piccadilly Station was soon outgrown. Charles Holden, perhaps Britain's most original architect of the twentieth century, designed the new circular concourse and booking office area, which opened in 1928. Located beneath Eros, subways reach out to all points of the Circus. The 'see how they run' device (panel of six dials to the right) recorded the train interval times on the Underground.

Southgate Station, c.1935. Opened on 13 March 1933, this is probably the most novel design of all London's underground stations. A ring of shops surrounds the circular booking office. The 'flying saucer' building was designed by C.H. James – Charles Holden is usually credited but was only used as a consultant here.

Cockfosters, 1933. Northern terminus of the Piccadilly line, this station was opened on 31 July 1933. The cathedral-like reinforced concrete train-shed, designed by Charles Holden, was the predecessor of the much more impressive one at Uxbridge.

The Tube Station, Edgware.

Edgware Station, c.1930. Edgware was reached by the first of the Underground's great forays into outermost suburbia on 18 August 1924. The building, designed by Stanley Heaps, imitates a Roman villa and was built of brick and Portland stone. The west wing (right), was demolished for the abandoned extension to Bushey Heath. The east wing (left) went in 1990 to be replaced by a more conveniently placed replica.

Uxbridge Station, c.1939. Opened on 4 December 1938, Uxbridge lies on the furthest outskirts of London. The building was designed by Charles Holden and L.H. Bucknell and is the only underground station in London with stained glass windows. The sculptures over the entrance are derived from upturned wheels and suspension leaf springs. It is served by Metropolitan and Piccadilly Line trains.

Five

The Tuppenny Tube

The Central London Railway opened on 30 July 1900 and initially ran between Shepherds Bush and Bank linking the western suburbs with the City and West End. Although not the first deep level underground electric railway ('tube'), the CLR – now the Central Line – was the one which struck the public imagination most fully and therefore was well illustrated on old postcards. The line was known as the 'Tuppenny Tube' because of its flat fare of two old pennies (2d) for journeys of any length. This universal fare was abolished in 1908 when all lines on the present Underground adopted a common fare structure.

In this section, a journey on the Central London is illustrated. Hopefully the views depicted here will recapture some of the novelty felt by travellers on the early tubes.

CENTRAL LONDON RAILWAY
TO THE
FRANCO-BRITISH EXHIBITION.

THE DIRECT LINE

Trains Run Every Few Minutes.

WEEKDAYS. FROM	FIRST TRAIN a.m.	LAST TRAIN a.m.
WOOD LANE (Exhibition)	5. 0	12. 5
BANK - - - -	5.20	12.30

SUNDAYS.	a.m.	p.m.
WOOD LANE (Exhibition)	8. 0	11.30
BANK - - - -	8.20	11.50

Average Time between Stations, 2 Minutes.

Post Office Station, c.1902. We begin our journey outside the station. The surface buildings of the early tubes were unremarkable and could easily be mistaken for shop fronts. Although functional there was a degree of decoration in a baroque style – each of the carved heads between the bays was different. This building was altered in 1929, gutted by fire in 1940 and demolished in 1948. The station has been called St Pauls since 1937.

Holland Park Station, c.1907. The street buildings on the Central London were generally single storied and to a standard pattern by Henry B. Measures. The Central London Railway had thirteen original stations, twelve with buildings. Six of them survive, including this example of the simplest type.

Notting Hill Gate Station, *c*.1908. For the more important stations a slightly more ornate design was used, featuring a cherub above an oval plaque. This building was demolished in 1959. Since then, a shared entrance to both the Central and Metropolitan line platforms was constructed.

Chancery Lane Station, *c*.1907. This station had the standard ground floor booking office building with facing in light brown ('biscuit') coloured stone, but here the upper floors of offices, of red brick and designed by Delissa Josephs are also present. A subsurface booking hall rendered this building obsolete in 1934 but it still exists and until recently was the entrance to a not-so-secret underground bunker.

Booking office at Bank Station, c.1902. Having entered the station we now have to buy our ticket. Tickets are available singly or in booklets from the counters to our left. Bank Station was unusual in that the booking office was underground and was entered from subways. The whole area was destroyed on 11 January 1941 when the roof collapsed after being struck by a bomb, creating the 'largest crater in London'.

Lifts at Bank Station, c.1902. Having bought our ticket and a paper we must now force our way to the lift. The crowd throngs around us; each style of hat denotes a particular social class. All early tubes possessed only lifts and stairs; escalators came later. Escalators replaced the four original lifts at Bank in 1924-1925. We deposit our tickets in the box provided (to the left of the man with the droopy moustache) and head for the lift.

Interior of Central London lift, c.1902. The doors are open and the smartly dressed lift-man, clutching the key used to operate the lift in his hand, ushers us inside. There were originally forty-nine electric lifts on the line, the last were replaced in the late 1970s. The gates were closed manually until around 1914 when compressed air began to be used. The descent takes a few seconds, the lift-man draws the doors back and we step out onto the platform.

Bank Station, c.1902. This is the typical white tiled platform of an early tube. The platform is wooden but there is complete electric lighting – a novelty in 1900. There are only three rails (as compared to four on the modern Underground) resting on longitudinal sleepers. The running rails have a bridge cross section, said to be necessary as the engineers found that the ordinary type left insufficient room for trains.

Central London locomotive, *c.1902*. Before our train arrives a locomotive rumbles through. The CLR used locomotives like this one for just three years before excessive noise and vibration led to the introduction of the more familiar multiple units. The General Electric Company of Schenectady, USA, built twenty-eight of these forty-four ton, camel-backed monsters for the CLR. The livery was 'Crimson Lake' (maroon) with gold lettering.

Interior of Central London carriage, *c.1902*. Our train arrives. The guard pulls open the gates at the ends of each carriage and we get on. The moquette upholstery and ornate lampshades provided the most luxurious ride of any of the early tubes. This carriage was exceptional as the Prince of Wales (later Edward VII) used it when he formally opened the line on 27 June 1900; ordinary cars had plain, not floral, patterned upholstery.

Wood Lane power station, c.1902. Our journey stops here but before we leave the 'Tuppenny Tube', a peek behind the scenes. The CLR like other early tubes generated its own electricity. The power station was at Wood Lane, opposite where the BBC stands today. The plant closed in 1928 and current was then taken from Lots Road

Wood Lane Junction, c.1925. On 3 August 1920 Central London trains were extended to Ealing Broadway over the Ealing & Shepherds Bush Railway, a goods only link opened in 1917. At Wood Lane Junction the CLR (with train to right) reverted to left hand running, via a flyover, then joined the GW goods line (left).

Six

London's Other Stations

This section gives a representative sample of London's stations. There are several different types of station considered here: former termini, those on main and branch lines – mainly based on commuter traffic – and those on radial routes – mostly used for freight. The latter have probably been the most vulnerable to closure. In 1900 there were around 240 'ordinary' stations (excluding the termini and those on tube lines) within the boundaries of the London County Council, then virtually the whole of the conurbation. Now, a hundred years later, only 160 or so of these are still open. Reasons for closure vary, but revolve around replacement (usually by nearby tube stations) and underuse.

Spa Road, *c.*1903 (ref: N 24). Spa Road could dubiously claim to be London's first terminus. Opened on 8 February 1836, it was the London end of the London & Greenwich (later part of the SER) until October. The station was rebuilt to the form shown here in 1901 and was closed as a wartime economy measure on 15 March 1915. The exterior survives virtually intact.

Ludgate Hill, *c.*1907 (ref: L 21). Opened as the LCDR's City terminus on 1 June 1865, Ludgate Hill's *raison d'être* was removed by the opening of Holborn Viaduct. Unlike most ex-termini, it did not become a goods depot, but survived because of the intensive suburban services from south London to the City over this line. Finally closed on 3 March 1929, the street building was demolished in 1990.

Catford, *c.*1904 (not on map). A rural idyll in the valley of the Ravensbourne! The LCDR was, perhaps, the most dependent on its suburban traffic, spreading all over south London. Some of its stations such as this example, on a cut-off line between Nunhead and Shortlands, were virtually adjacent to those of other lines – in this case the SER's Catford Bridge (ref: U 28). Opened on 1 July 1892, these buildings lasted until 1970.

Lordship Lane, *c.*1910 (ref: U 24). Another of the Chatham's suburban ventures was its Crystal Palace line. Opened on 1 September 1865 Lordship Lane was in direct competition with Forest Hill. The handsome red brick and stone booking office building was a casualty of the 1939-1945 war. The line was never well used, partly because of the semi-rural surroundings, and closed on 20 September 1954.

Forest Hill, c.1935 (ref: U 25). The southern suburban network also included stations on the main lines. Forest Hill, on the Brighton main line, had a vigorous commuter trade. Opened on 3 June 1839, the up-side station buildings seen here dated from 1881 and were severely damaged by a flying bomb on 23 June 1944. The LBSCR was notable for the fine architecture of its London stations.

Vauxhall, c.1904 (ref: P 20). As well as serving suburbia the southern lines also had stations in gritty industrial areas. The first stop out of Waterloo on the LSWR main line, Vauxhall, opened on 11 July 1848. The station buildings were rebuilt to the form shown here after a fire in April 1856 and are still in use. In a roundabout way, Vauxhall gave the Russians their word for station!

Clapton, *c.*1905 (ref: E 25). North of the river only the Great Eastern had an extensive commuter network, mainly because, like the southern companies, it had no substantial industrial traffic. London's north eastern suburbs were opened up towards the end of the last century. Served by Chingford branch trains, and opened on 1 July 1872, Clapton is typical. Only part of the station building still exists, the rest being rebuilt in 1983.

Stoke Newington, *c.*1910 (ref: E 24). Opened on 27 May 1872, the design of this station is characteristic of those on the GER's principal suburban routes – hard-wearing brick with simple gothic details. The station buildings were demolished some years ago and replaced by a large glass booking hall. The shops on the left remain but now house a Caribbean takeaway and a taxi firm.

Canning Town, *c.*1905 (ref: K 30). As well as its suburban holdings the GER made full use of the docks which lay within its domain. The line to North Woolwich was well used by goods traffic but also had a working class passenger clientele. Canning Town, an original station on the line, opened on 14 June 1847. This building dated from 1888 and was demolished in 1932.

Silvertown, *c.*1910 (not on map). Also on the North Woolwich branch, this station opened on 19 June 1863 and is typical of the work-a-day appearance of the stations that served London's once-thriving docks. Taken from a public footbridge, one of London's few level crossings can be seen in the foreground. The station and signal box remained as seen until fairly recently but the level crossing was abolished some years ago.

Coburn Road, *c.*1906 (ref: I 27). The GER also had considerable traffic on its main line. However, in the inner area it ran through one of the poorest parts of London – stations here were therefore not well used. Opened on 1 February 1863 and resited in 1883, Coburn Road was closed on 8 December 1946 due to depopulation and to the opening of new tube stations. Ridge and furrow awning with 'dragon's teeth' valancing was very common on the GER.

Lea Bridge, *c.*1900 (ref: E 27). The Great Eastern had a second – more exactly a wannabe – mainline. This was one of the original stops on the Northern & Eastern Railway to Cambridge, which opened on 15 September 1840. The early booking office building above the line was irreparably damaged by fire in 1944, although not as a result of enemy action. The platform buildings went in the 1970s but the station remained open until 8 July 1985.

Ealing Broadway, *c.*1930 (ref: K 5). Across the capital and in contrast the Great Western showed little inclination to develop its suburban services which were limited almost exclusively to its main line. One of the most important stations, Ealing Broadway, was opened on 1 December 1838. This building, not the original, is a typical Great Western design with short pavilion towers crowned with metal work. It was demolished in 1966.

West Ealing, *c.*1910 (ref: L 3). One stop down the line, this station, originally Castle Hill, opened on 1 March 1871. The original booking office building, seen here, has some similarity to Royal Oak and has been replaced in recent years. The information board bears journey times to Paddington (eighteen minutes), the City (thirty-five minutes via the Met) and Victoria (forty minutes via the West London).

Greenford, *c*.1910 (not on map). Like the Great Eastern, the GWR also had a second mainline. This was the 'Birmingham cut-off'. Despite being a shorter route and engineered for higher speeds the line never took off and its London section was adopted by the Underground. When first opened, on 1 October 1904, this station – one of the earliest on the line – was completely surrounded by countryside yet today the area is definitely urban in character. Rendered obsolete by a Central Line replacement, it was closed in 1963. The street level building, a standard GWR design, has been integrated into a new structure on the site.

Highgate, *c.*1910 (ref: C 18). The other 'Great' with extensive commuter services was the Great Northern. Suburban traffic seemed an embarrassment to the GNR, which contracted out to the North London. The most important GNR suburban lines were the Northern Heights branches. These centred on Highgate, which opened on 22 August 1867. Traces of the original side platforms can be seen.

Highgate, 1938 (ref: C 18). This view of the booking office building was taken in connection with plans to electrify the line and join it to the ex-GNCR tube. The station was rebuilt for this scheme, which unfortunately never came to fruition. The Northern Line station lies below the site and effectively replaced the ex-GNR station, which closed on 5 July 1954. The old station remains virtually intact.

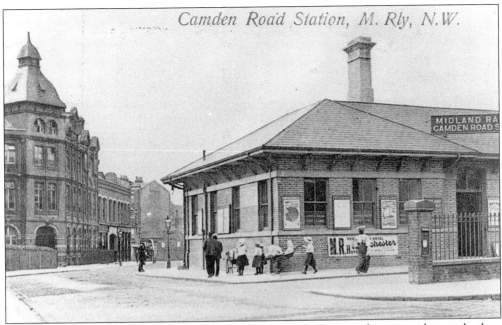

Camden Road, *c*.1910 (ref: G 19). The Midland was the least enthusiastic about suburban services of all the main line companies. The company never promoted its London services, relying instead on its lucrative long distance passenger and goods trade. First station out of St Pancras on the Midland main line, Camden Road opened on 13 July 1868 and was closed on 1 January 1916 primarily as a result of tram competition.

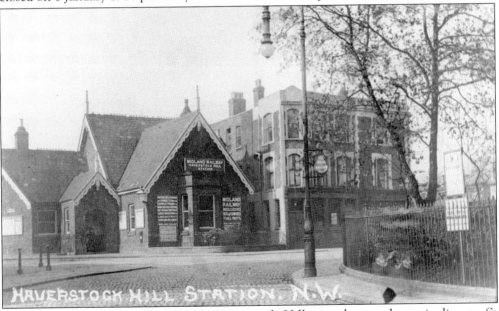

Haverstock Hill, *c*.1910 (ref: F 17). Haverstock Hill was also on the main line to St Pancras and, like Camden Road, opened on 13 July 1868 and closed on 1 January 1916. The booking office building, with its ornate bargeboards, was a special effort for a once genteel neighbourhood. This remained until the 1960s when it was demolished following a fire.

Dudding Hill, *c.*1910 (ref: F 10). Although the Midland had no suburban branch lines in London, it had interests in several lines which concentrated on goods work. This station, opened on 3 August 1875, was on the line from Cricklewood to Acton, which gave the Midland access to the southern companies. The line's passenger services were not well patronized and were withdrawn on 1 October 1902. The buildings survived until 1989.

Junction Road, *c.*1910 (ref: F 19). The Midland was also involved in the Tottenham & Hampstead Joint, which gave it access to the docks. Junction Road, the second station out from Kentish Town, opened on 1 January 1872. Although passenger services continue on the line, trains ceased to call here on 3 May 1943, primarily because of the proximity of Tufnell Park tube station. The platform buildings were demolished in the 1950s.

Uxbridge Road, *c.*1910 (ref: M 12). GWR, LNWR, Metropolitan and NLR trains provided services over the West London Railway, then as now an important goods link. This station, with a street building of LNWR pattern, opened on 1 November 1869. It closed on 19 October 1940 due to wartime economies. The site was cleared for road improvements around 1971. A door-to-door milk seller pushes his cart past the front of the station.

Gunnersbury, *c.*1910 (ref: O 7). Opened on 1 January 1869 as Brentford Road, this station was built for the LSWR trains to Kensington which ceased in 1916. At one time the trains of as many as seven companies stopped here. Formerly LNWR, LSWR, Midland, Metropolitan and GWR services used the station. North London and District trains continue to do so. This building was pulled down in 1967 for the current mess.

The Scenic Railway, Franco-British Exhibition, London, 1908

Scenic railway station, White City, 1908. A bit of a departure here. The scenic railway was the most popular attraction at the White City exhibition in Shepherds Bush, carrying nearly three million passengers during the 1908 season alone. Opened for the Franco-British exhibition of 1908, the railway remained in use until it was dismantled during the First World War.

"WILD GOOSE" THE FAR TOTTERING AND OYSTERCREEK RAILWAY, FESTIVAL GARDENS, FESTIVAL OF BRITAIN 1951.   EV.31.

Wild Goose at Oystercreek Station, 1951. While we are on the subject of pleasure railways, it is worth illustrating one of the most famous. This is the 15in gauge Far Tottering & Oystercreek Railway in the Festival of Britain Pleasure Gardens, Battersea Park, created to the designs of cartoonist Rowland Emmett, who drew for 'Punch'.

Seven

North Western Suburban

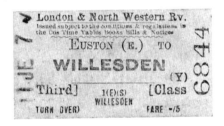

The London and Birmingham Railway was the first main line to London, opening from Euston to Boxmoor on 20 July 1837 and through to Birmingham the following year. In 1846 the company combined with several others to form the London & North Western Railway. Calling itself 'the Premier Line', the North Western was the largest and wealthiest in Britain. Like most lines that concentrated mainly on long distance traffic suburban services were slow to develop. Nevertheless, by the end of the First World War an extensive and well-established suburban network existed centred on Willesden Junction. To aid in its further development a new electrified line exclusively for local services was built running parallel to the existing railway. This was the 'New Line' which was completed in 1922 and was also served by Bakerloo trains.

These views portray some of the stations and important features, which could be seen on the Euston to Willesden Junction section of the LNWR.

Camden bank, c.1905. This view has changed in detail but the multiplicity of lines passing above and below each other is typical of the railway scene between Euston and Primrose Hill – or indeed the approach to any of the main line termini. In the foreground the line to the left, used for empty stock workings, passes below the running lines. On the right a suburban train passes the side of a carriage shed.

Construction near Camden Town, 1836. Seventy years earlier this engraving was made from an identical viewpoint – Mornington Street Bridge. Building a railway during the Victorian age was truly a Herculean task. Carried out using only simple tools, the work was mostly done by Irish navvies. Park Street (now Parkway) Bridge is the common element in both views and was rebuilt when the main line was electrified in the 1960s.

Primrose Hill Tunnel, 1836. Primrose Hill is the first tunnel on the line. At 3,492ft long and 22ft wide, it took eight millions bricks to build. This is the original appearance of the south portal, which was designed by a Mr Budden. Special architectural treatment was merited as the railway passed through a good neighbourhood. The drawing is by John Bourne who recorded many scenes of the construction and original features of the L&BR.

Primrose Hill Tunnel, 1923. This is the much less picturesque northern end of the tunnel. Further tunnels were added in 1879 and 1922. Steam pours from the original mouth on the right proclaiming the passage of an express. The metal bridge takes the GCR lines over the LNWR. The platforms of South Hampstead are in the foreground.

Loudoun Road Station, c.1905 (ref: H 15). This station, now South Hampstead and the first out from Euston, opened on 2 June 1879. The clap boarded booking office building with Tudor style chimneys was rather fine and fitted in well with its surroundings. A similar example was once to be found at Wolverton in Buckinghamshire, but both have now sadly vanished.

South Hampstead Station, 1923 (ref: H 15). Temporarily closed during the First World War, Loudoun Road reopened in 1922 as South Hampstead. This is looking north towards the back of the booking office. The platforms to the right are on the 'New Line'. To the left are the now abandoned slow line platforms. The covered stairway and some platform buildings remain.

Kilburn High Road, *c*.1910 (ref: H 14). Opened in July 1852, the station stands on the site of 'Kilbourn Wells', an early spa. A 4-4-0 heads an express travelling south to Euston on the main line. On the local line platforms to the right stands a train, probably of NLR origins. The station has been rebuilt but the domed building visible in the centre is still a familiar feature for those who travel this line.

McVities siding, Willesden, *c*.1905. These sidings, for supply of raw material and removal of finished products, were typical of those throughout the capital. This is the biscuit works of the famous McVities. The railway no longer serves the factory although track survives in this area. The smell of baking still permeates trains speeding past the area.

Willesden Junction Station, *c.*1905 (ref: I 10). Willesden has had a station on this line since around 1842, but the current site came into use on 1 August 1866. The street building, with its polychromatic brickwork, opened on 12 August 1894 and was part of a comprehensive reconstruction. Backing on to the main line, the booking office remained in use until demolished for alterations in the Millennium year.

Willesden Junction Station, *c.*1895 (ref: I 10). These are the main platforms looking south. To the right a double headed express heads north, while on the left is a local line train at the end of its run. The back of the booking hall building can be seen to the far left. In the foreground Old Oak Lane passes over the railway. The platforms seen here ceased to be used in 1962. Their site has been almost completely cleared.

WILLSDEN TRAIN SMASH DEC 1910.

Train smash at Willesden Junction Station, 1910. At 8.55 a.m. on 5 December 1910 the 8.30 Watford to Broad Street slammed into the rear of the 8.27 Watford to Euston. The last two coaches of the latter 'telescoped' killing five people and injuring over seventy more. The Broad Street train had been cleared by signals – signalman George Blundell had pulled the wrong lever. The inquest returned a verdict of accidental death.

Stonebridge Park power station, 1914. The plant was built for the electrification of LNWR inner suburban services for which a new set of tracks was laid down from Euston to Watford – the 'New Line'. LNWR electric services also ran to Broad Street, on the West London Railway to Kensington, and to Richmond via the N&SWJR. The mighty edifice shown here has been demolished.

New Line train, c.1925. The 'New Line' electrification was compatible with the Underground and Bakerloo trains began to use the line early in 1915. This type, owned jointly by the LMS and the Underground, was delivered in 1920 and was designed for through running onto the tube. The early trains on this line were remarkably luxurious – a contrast to today's wretched boneshakers.

Eight

Behind the Scenes

Not all railway activity was immediately obvious. Goods traffic being a case in point. Britain's railways were built as much for goods as passengers so the provision of facilities was vital. Several different types are depicted including goods depots, marshalling yards and goods only lines. This traffic has now virtually disappeared due to the shifting of cargo to the roads – neither an inevitable or beneficial process. Although London never had as many as the north, several private industrial railways existed, mainly dealing with specialized goods traffic. Other behind the scenes work includes the routine maintenance and housing of rolling stock and track carried out from the Depots. Another major activity was the manufacture and repair of locomotives and rolling stock. Districts of every major city were dominated by this activity: Stratford was London's 'railway town'. Working without widespread recognition and with long hours and poor pay railwaymen got a poor deal but without them the railways could not run at all. The public was also seldom witness to the construction of the railways.

Fleet Street railway offices, 1930. Once a feature of every High Street, such offices were partly for enquiries and purchasing tickets but also served as collection and distribution points for parcels and small goods. The offices pictured here had the main entrance at 64 Fleet Street (top) and a side entrance in Bouverie Street (bottom). They were built in 1930.

Horse-drawn goods cart, Savoy Hill, 1892. Surprisingly one of the key parts of the traditional railway goods system was not rail bound at all. The horse-drawn cart was used to pick up and deliver goods on a door-to-door basis. Such carts would usually be based at one of the large goods stations. This example was owned by the Great Northern Railway and is seen at the back of the Savoy Hotel. The driver was one W. Stacey.

Paddington goods station, c.1900. Heavily laden horse-drawn railway goods wagons were once a common sight in the capital. Opened in 1858 on the site of the 'temporary' passenger station, this depot was rebuilt in the 1920s, closed in 1975 and has now almost completely vanished. The warehouse frontage to the sheds is to the left in the background.

Bishopsgate goods station, c.1925 (ref: J 23). Railways are ideal for shifting heavy loads over long distances. Traditional goods traffic, however, consisted of small items carried over short distances. Huge sorting facilities were required, such as the set up shown here. The Great Eastern's Shoreditch station was converted into a goods depot in 1882. Burnt down on 5 December 1964, it is now a car park.

Kings Cross goods station, 1853. In addition to road to rail transfer, most railway companies also desired access to the Regents Canal. The transit sheds at Kings Cross housed all three under one roof. In addition the Granary, a six-storey grain warehouse, provided excellent storage capacity. Lewis Cubbitt designed the well-planned layout. The Granary remains in its original condition but the transit sheds have been extensively altered.

Bricklayers Arms goods station, c.1905 (ref: N 23). Like most of the big goods depots Bricklayers Arms was a former passenger terminus. Originally opened as the SER's 'Grand West-End Terminus' on 1 May 1844, it was given over to freight in 1852. This is the Swansgate entrance. To the left is the turret of Lewis Cubbitt's original frontage, which was destroyed by fire in 1936. Closed for goods in 1977, the site has been cleared.

Goods train, Clapham Junction, *c.*1950 (ref: R 16). British Railways No.44909 leaves Platform 17 on a freight from the West London line. The primary element of railway goods work was of course the regular goods train. The wooden wagons, then in common use, have long since vanished.

Ferme Park yards, *c.*1910. Long lines of goods wagons were commonplace in Britain until the 1960s. These yards were opened in 1888 and were located to the east and west of the GNR mainline between Haringay and Hornsey (ref: C21) stations. To the right an 0-6-0 saddle tank on light goods duties stands on the well used down relief line (known to engine-men as 'the cab rank'). The yards mostly closed between 1966 and 1968.

Silvertown tramway, c.1912. The extent of goods traffic often required freight only lines, such as the 'Silvertown Tramway'. In 1855 the opening of the Royal Victoria Dock severed the original GER route to North Woolwich. Part continued in goods use serving riverside factories. The new passenger line and the high walled descent to a tunnel, necessitated by further dock development, can be seen to the right of the church.

Deptford lift bridge, c.1905. The LBSCR line to Deptford Wharf opened on 2 July 1849 and was a 1½ mile long goods-only branch from New Cross (ref: P 26) to the Thames. The bridge, the only one of its type in southern England, could be raised to permit the passage of barges on the Grand Surrey Canal. The branch was closed in 1963 and the canal filled in around the same time.

Royal Arsenal Railway, Woolwich, c.1915. 'This is the little train inside the Arsenal in which we go down from the college to the danger area... You can see the men sat further along and the carriage is reserved for officers and ladies.' (message on reverse). The Woolwich Arsenal, main ammunition manufacturing centre of Great Britain, had an extensive narrow gauge (18in) and standard gauge network. *Phoenix*, an 0-4-0 saddle tank built in 1901, leads a narrow-gauge train. This type was the workhorse of the RAR.

Sydenham gasworks, *c.*1950. Most gasworks had internal systems. The largest was at Beckton but Sydenham was more typical. The Bell Green works had three miles of track and was accessible from the SER's Mid Kent line near Lower Sydenham Station (ref: W 27). The plant closed in the late 1960s. *Anne*, an 0-4-0 saddle tank, bears the initials of the South Suburban Gas Company but this view was taken after nationalization.

Port of London Authority train, *c.*1910. The Port of London Authority (PLA) was formed in 1909 to control London's docks. The PLA owned many miles of track, particularly in the Royal Docks. Trains, typically drawn by the 0-6-0 tank type loco seen here, were largely for internal goods movements. However, special passenger trains for ships at the docks as well as for workmen were also run.

Cricklewood locomotive sheds, *c*.1910. Cricklewood (near Cricklewood Station ref: E 12) was one of two Midland Railway locomotive depots in London. A roundhouse was opened in 1882, and a second in 1893. A large number of well polished engines are arrayed around the turntable. Underneath the locos are inspection pits while above are extractors to remove fumes from inside the shed. Steam engines ceased to use the shed in 1964.

Peckham Rye depot, *c*.1910. This carriage shed – near Peckham Rye Station (ref: Q 24) – was built for the electrification scheme of the LBSCR. Known as the Elevated Electric, the first section was inaugurated in 1909. These petrol driven rail-motors were acquired to maintain the overhead apparatus. The overhead lines were converted to third rail in 1928-1929. The depot no longer exists.

Stratford Works, *c.*1913. Stratford Locomotive and Carriage Works (ref: H 29) opened in the 1840s and eventually occupied over 100 acres. Stratford New Town was built for GER works employees and was known as 'Hudson's Town' after the famous 'Railway King'. The works ceased to make locomotives in 1924 and this site has been completely cleared. This is the No.2 Gate ('Loco gate') in Angel Lane.

Stratford works, *c.*1910. 'Swarm of bees that settled on boiler (firebox foundation ring) outside new engine repair shop' (caption on back of original). This view confirms the statement that the Edwardians would make a postcard of anything. Oddly enough the surreal combination of nature and human engineering was popular at this time and several similar examples are known.

Station staff at Leytonstone, *c.*1910. The unsung heroes of the railways. This fine view unfortunately could not be dated – does any reader know when the royal teacups were stolen? Leytonstone (ref: D 30) was an original stop on the GER line to Loughton, Epping and Ongar, which opened on 22 August 1856. Rebuilt for the coming of the Central Line in 1947, there is no trace of the old buildings at platform level.

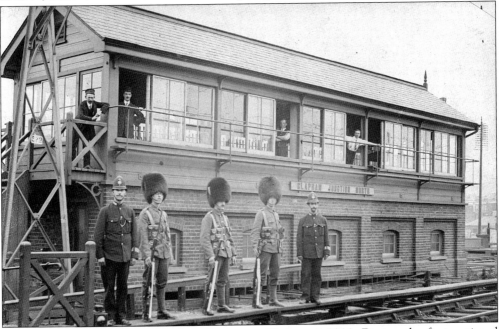

Protecting strike-breakers, Clapham Junction, 19 August 1911. During the first national rail strike troops supplemented the police to protect blacklegs from violence – the action was generally peaceful but turned nasty in places. The results, in terms of improvements in wages and conditions, were inconclusive. This is the LBSCR's North (later 'B') signal box located near the station (ref: R 16). Built in 1910, it was replaced in 1952.

Construction of St Johns Wood tunnels, 1897. The Manchester, Sheffield & Lincoln Railway's extension from Nottingham to Marylebone opened in 1899. To commemorate its completion the MS&L became the Great Central. Because of the great expense to an already hard pressed company wits said that 'Money Sunk and Lost' had 'Gone Completely'. 'The Clog and Knocker', as the Great Central was affectionately known, has now indeed gone completely – only a tiny suburban remnant still exists of the last main line. In the background is St Johns Wood Station (ref: J 16) on the Metropolitan and the church of St John the Baptist. This picture will interest cricket fans – this is Lord's! The turf was dug up then carefully replaced with no interruption to matches.